For My Robbie-

    I will love you forever and ever and ever again…

    "Every Love Story is Beautiful But Ours is

        My Favorite"

For My Grandson Duke-

  Always Remember

  Your Grandma Brandi Loves You

  Very Very Much.

Entry One - Alone … The beginning of grief, the depth of love, & the birth of reinvention.	5
Entry 2 - Arts, Crafts, & Coping	13
Entry 3 - Living In an Art Studio Vs. A Cabin Home	16
Entry 4 - What My Animals Taught Me	18
Entry 5 - When Some Things Seem Like a Good Idea	21
Entry 6 - The Bear Part One & The Bear Part Two	26
Entry 7 - You Can Take the Girl Out of Seattle, But You Can't Take Seattle Out of the Girl	34
Entry 8 - Weird Things I Have Found On My Porch	36
Entry 9 - Fear of Birds… Aviary PTSD is REAL	39
Entry 10 - There Is a Mouse In My House	45
Entry 11 - The Invasion	47
Entry 12 - The Ark	49
Entry 13 - The Weight On One Set of Hands	58
Entry 14 - Grief Is Not a Straight Line	65
Entry 15 - Summary, Notes on Survival With a Soapbox Closer…	71
Entry 16 - About the Author	76

Entry One - Alone … The beginning of grief, the depth of love, & the birth of reinvention.

There are days when the quiet is deafening. There are days it screams.

When the memories are so present there is no way to escape them- tangible at times in the form of an Anniversary card, photo, concert ticket, or a million other happy triggers or tragic rabbit holes. My heart presses so hard against my chest I think it is breaking all over again and my head might split from the pressure of the pain.

When being alone isn't peaceful or brave—it's just alone.

When I sat in my chair without Rob sitting next to me those first days, I stared at his empty chair and wanted desperately to see him filling it. But….no, he would never sit next to me in that chair again. I thought about it. I still think about it. I still talk to him, in my head and out loud, especially when I am forced to do something that would have fallen under his jurisdiction. I do talk to him—out loud. There is no response of course, I just imagine what he would say then either smile, or shake my head depending.

We were married five days short of 20 years. ALS took him from me. It is a cruel, vicious disease. He had a form called Bulbar ALS which basically starts at end stages - loss of speech, muscle deterioration, inability to expel carbon dioxide, inability to swallow, and so much more. The person I loved who was larger than life, always moving, and getting things done. If he had an idea - he followed through, always. Then seeing the frustration of not being able to count on his body, as it failed him bit by bit, was awful.

His love for me was absolute.

The fact that his mind stayed sharp was a blessing and a curse. His sense of humor was still there - he just had to write down his one liners instead of speaking them to me.

One of the most vivid and painful memories was when I came home early from a meeting, crying because I felt so alone without him there by my side. He stood up, which took so much effort, and held me as we both cried - feeling cheated of the future we had planned. He told me he wasn't ready to leave me and I told him I wasn't ready to say goodbye.

Care-giving is the most difficult thing you can do and something that loved ones never would ask from us, but the ultimate gift of love we can give. I am so very thankful that I was able to do that for him, the final gift I could give him. When he passed, he was home, in his chair, in the cabin. I was able to hold his hand and assure him of my love in those final moments. His physical suffering had ended and I was alone, facing 'our' future together, by myself. Along with the feeling of immense loss, is the anger of feeling that we were cheated of our plans and that our story ended way too soon.

Alone means you don't have to take into consideration what the other person wants to watch, or listen to. I have not watched his two favorite movies -Wyatt Earp or Dances With Wolves. Eat when you want- eat what you want. Go to bed and wake up according to your schedule.

I started going to bed at pm -yep, early. My rationalization is that once I go to bed - the day is done. If I make it to that time, I've lived through another day, tackled whatever came my way and lived.

A psychological trick, and you are welcome to borrow it. String enough days together and it's a week, then a month, then a year, etc…

We always had a furry family. When we moved to Montana we had 3 dogs and 2 cats. Through our first years here we lost two to age. That left one - Annie.

"The PHLOYD"

Our two cats, Phrank and Phloyd out lived him. Phloyd we had for 19 years - that cat was smart! He knew when you needed comfort, or a laugh and was happy to provide either. Phrank adopted us.

Our first winter here, I went out to the back porch to get something from the freezer- a cat jumped from the top of the freezer on me. Random cats are few and far between in Montana - outside cats don't last long.

Welcome Phrank to our family. He was our mouser, he had two front fangs like a saber tooth tiger. He didn't mess around - one bite and it was bye bye mouse.

Disposing of the mice was always Rob's job. Phrank would take the mouse to where Rob was as drop it. Rob would pick it up (with tissue) and go into the commode room to give it a watery burial. Phrank would stand on his hind feet and watch the mouse go down. Then BINGO - he got a can of wet cat food as his reward, this arrangement worked for a few years. The first time he came and dropped a mouse in front of me- there was not enough tissue in the house for me to pick that thing up. I did some yelling at Rob as I dashed

"PHRANK - The Mouse King

to flush the latest fatality. Thankfully we only have a few a year (still too many)!

Annie was his dog, 500%. She tolerated me, still does. We have reached a truce - its taken over 5 years. That girl will still walk the opposite direction if I call her. A leash and harness are my friends. Annie still misses Rob. Evidenced by the fact that whenever a diesel truck comes up the driveway, she instantly perks up like -"Rob's home!". But, of course, he's not.

Annie - Rob's Dog

One thing that no one tells you, but, you should know, is that no matter how you feel, sick, tired, headache, depressed, etc… You MUST get up. Not because you want to, but because animals don't care about grief. They care about food, a clean cat box, scratching posts and schedules. They make you move and go through the steps. Many days I am thankful for them - sometimes, not so much.

Alone in this cabin, I've learned that grief, as fluid as it is for each of us, is love, with nowhere to go. That the quiet isn't empty—it's just full of everything I miss

Sometimes, I whisper into the silence

"I miss you.

My heart answers back - "I miss you too"

"Rob & Me"

Entry 2 - Arts, Crafts, & Coping

Entry Two: Arts, Crafts and Coping

If you were to ask my best friend Kathy- she would tell you that I have been known to do some serious damage with dead flowers and a glue gun - not to mention painting palm trees, complete with coconuts in gold paint. Let me say, setting me loose in a craft store was my vibe.)

Losing Rob put me in a tailspin of artistic epic experimenting. Starting with my hair.

I always had short highlighted hair for most of my life - It was thin and fine - but, it covered my head. So, I was set to go in for a trim and I started perusing Pintrist. Talk about a rabbit hole. I was ready for some kind of change.

It was the beginning of the COVID outbreak - things were shutting down, people were paranoid (with cause), so, being "alone" took on a life of its own. I saw this woman with gorgeous short hair is was a brown base with lavender tones - beautiful. I was looking forward to looking like the picture. No matter how many times I tell myself that my hair is incapable of certain achievements, "hope springs eternal". Apparently this color change was one of these incapable feats.

I had a white - not silver base color and a neon lavender "highlight" - the highlight became the main color. It was an epic Pintrist fail.

After really stopping and taking stock of my appearance I was not only depressed because of Rob, but, I was the heaviest I had ever been. Bad self esteem combination.

Zoom started to figure heavily in my social life as that was how my religious meetings were being held. When my hair was purple and thin I wore thick headbands and tried to keep it at a low profile.

I turned 50 years old and made a decision. There was no way I was going to be able to grow thick hair - it kept getting thinner, but it turned curly after being stick straight my whole life.

Stress + Loss + Medications + Post Menopause all will curl and thin out even the healthiest, straightest of hair- it did.

So, I subsequently decided that I was going to buy the hair I always wanted. Whatever color, length, straight/wavy hair appealed to me - there was a wig that fit the bill. Most people try to match their own hairstyle or type - not me! Red, blonde, the lavender color I had wanted, brunette, black, curly - straight - I tried all of them. You can get some great starter wigs on Amazon for under $20. That made it feasible - shelling out a few hundred per wig wasn't in my greatly restricted budget.

Polymer clay became my medium of choice for the duration of COVID. I made all different types of flowers, beads, hearts - jewelry made with wire, crystals, beads and clay. I made literally a ton of all of those. Really poured my heart, no pun intended, into working with my hands and working with all different colors. In a gray winter- color was vital to add in. I posted photography for sale on a couple different sites. Tried watercolors. Filled up at least ten adult coloring books - mandala patterns mostly - I think I used every single color of sparkle gel pens. Working with color. Very important for me - in fact, it was vital. Being a visual person - enjoying different patterns and colors was very helpful.

What I was creating needed to be financially helpful. Making ends meet was a monthly challenge.

I sold some photography note cards, a few canvas prints, but, I was rapidly becoming a starving artist with a weight issue.

Welcome to the world of multi level marketing, I joined a magnetic lash company and was moderately successful. They emphasized social media and selfies.

I took my wigs, slapped on lashes and snapped pics, tik toc videos, Instagram, Facebook posts and live clips. Editing pictures was my strong suit. Oh, and lip-syncing tik tocs - lots of clips marketing product. People being stuck at home made them more open to try lashes, when they couldn't get out and see their lash techs - it filled a niche. Playing dress up, being someone else for a few minutes, erasing my double chin with the editing filter - smoothed out skin and ta dah -instant (sort of) Glam.

During that time, I did Avon, Scentsy, Party lite, and the Lash Company. Needless to say, I ended up investing in those far more than making a profit. Etsy was not the platform that worked for me - plus the costs and renewing listings, etc… was not cost effective. I still have my Etsy account but, it is barely a representation of what I do. I tried blogging, writing poetry and short stories…I had some interest, but certainly no viral moments.

The platform that has consistently helped me mostly eliminate the gap between ends every month. I have actively worked my Poshmark closet for several of the past years and it has really helped my cash flow - Financial Freedom is not even close but, a little less financial stress is always welcome.

I am no longer a selfie junkie, and I don't play dress up like I used to. But, selling things on line is still part of my life. I have posted some of my art on there, as a litmus test. So far so good.

Just within the last couple months I have created my own website. It's a bit of a work in progress but, I am pretty proud of it. (www.brandisgart.com)

I recently have been taking an AI class and wow. It can help do practically anything. One thing to keep in mind is it loves to take poetic license with dictation. This book was no exception. It created entries and events that never occurred. Hence, I have re-written this book myself - it is an accurate account. I am proud of that.

Entry 3 - Living In an Art Studio Vs. A Cabin Home

As I mentioned previously, I'm a visual person. Like, if it is out of my reach or line of sight - it doesn't exist.

It got to the point that there was a path through the cabin - bed to kitchen to bathroom / laundry room. We have one (1) closet in the whole house for both of us. Like I said storage is a premium around here. All of Rob's things were in his "side of the closet" or stacked around the cabin. I couldn't bring myself to address those things for over a year.

I have a brilliant person who has helped me navigate shark infested waters for some years now. Not only my therapist, but, a dear friend. Rob greatly respected her and asked her to stay a regular part of my life - she agreed and has been a pillar through all of this.

I would jokingly tell people that I lived in an art studio, it was just me, so, it was everything I wanted to do at my fingertips- literally. (Including a ton of yarn projects that I was crocheting - afghans, scarves, hats, all the things.)

One day, I was on the phone with my therapist and she said take a picture of my coffee table and send it to her. Like that minute. I was embarrassed but, I did. I knew the clutter was out of control, there were souvenirs from every trip Rob and I had ever taken. Boxes of my clay creations/jewelry. Tons of photos to turn into photography note cards. Lots of books on every topic by my "go to" authors. I went through a Kindle obsession with Pride and Prejudice inspired novels - it's a real genre, who knew? I went through those novels like candy. It was so nice to see Elizabeth Bennett and Mr. Darcy beyond Jane Austen. Between reading sappy novels and Hallmark Movies - the most sugary sweet… escapism at it's finest.

Back to the coffee table…So, I took the photo and sent it as requested. There was no judgment - just a suggestion that I get the coffee table cleared off before we met the following week. Eating the elephant (clutter) one bite at a time. It took a lot of time - some backward steps, and ultimately more forward steps - caused a irrefutable win in the world of organization. It even progressed to the point that I was able to host my Mom and Sister for a visit the following Fall.

So that is the coffee table clearing story that launched a thousand organizational challenges and successes.

Entry 4 - What My Animals Taught Me

After Rob died, the animals knew before I told them.

Annie, his dog, was confused at first. She ran to the door, excited, whenever a truck pulled up our driveway. She looked at me every time I came home, checking to see if Rob was behind me.

Annie couldn't hide her disappointment. She waited on the porch, staring down the driveway, watching and listening intently. Her ears perked at every sound, even though we both knew his voice would no longer be heard and his distinctive footsteps had fallen silent for good.

Phloyd, a huge Russian Blue cat we had rescued years before we moved here, became the ultimate "Comfort King". He was always present - looking at me with those kind eyes. Sleeping with a low purr, that sound is one of the most underrated therapy tools I have ever come across. Phrank kept right on hunting for invaders of any kind. Annie slept curled up with Rob's pillow. As for me, I had to decide which side of the bed to sleep on.

Annie suddenly became my shadow out in the yard. (Unless I was trying to get her to come in - then the 'keep away' game commenced- Oy). We all shifted. The whole home dynamic shifted. The entire energy of the cabin was numb. We had a few months to prepare for the inevitable, but, nothing compares to the reality of such a significant loss.

There's a look animals get when they're trying to understand what we want, or need, from them. It's not confusion—it's processing. Watching Annie figure out that he was gone, really gone, gave us something in common. We formed an alliance of sorts. She knew what her job was, Rob told her to take care of me. She did and keeps continuing to do just that.

Rob had always taken Annie whenever he went anywhere. Her and I didn't have that kind of relationship - my Honda Pilot was a lot less dog friendly than Rob's big truck.

Then one day, I said to her "I'm going to the post office", (it's weird how you talk out loud to your pets, and then expect them to understand) - but, understand she did.

For the first time, she trotted over to me, and sat patiently by the passenger door. I grabbed an old towel and put it over the seat. Then I thought "Well, let's see if I am getting the point of this new behavior" . I opened the passenger door and easy as pie she hopped in and sat on the seat like she had called "shotgun". Her look said "Uh.. are we leaving?". Far be it from me to miss this bonding experience.

She was ready for a new routine. From that point on going to the post office has been our thing. Maybe I'd learn to drive like Rob did, I have to admit I am not even close. He was a great driver - me, not so much. Something definitely shifted in Annie and I's relationship that day, it was a new routine we were creating - whether we wanted to or not.

We did it, baby steps…

I've learned that grief isn't exclusive to the human heart. It lives in animals too. There is a reason people have support animals. Feelings show up in the silence, in the eyes, a purr - filling in the routines that now have gaps.

But I've also learned something else of note: Animals don't get stuck the way we do. They feel it, they move forward, able to shift focus and attention to where it is most needed. They don't deny sadness or drown in it. They adjust.

My furry family showed me to move forward we need to respect the life we previously lived, then put one foot in front of the other towards our new existence.

Our beloved animals didn't ask for the job, but they take it on anyway. Little therapists with fur and claws, being an unconditional presence and giving us love.

I'm still learning the whole adjusting portion- but, I am trying.

Entry 5 - When Some Things Seem Like a Good Idea

There's something about grief that makes you think about what the other person wanted and like a final gift, we make, maybe not the most practical of decisions … but, impractical and impetuous ones.

In my case, I figured a carport might fix everything.

Rob always wanted one. We have two massive 40-foot shipping containers sitting parallel with 40 feet between them. A large space by anyone's standards. He'd stand out there with his hands on his hips, staring at that gap like it was a crossword puzzle waiting to be solved - it was more like advanced Sudoku.

Rob researched, measured, stared, and went through every idea you could imagine. Finances were an issue so, that made him all the more creative. At one point, he even considered putting sod on top- packing it between criss-crossing logs, like some thing from the old west kind, or an Eco-mountain garage. I remember just looking at him trying to gauge how serious this idea was. Oh, he was very serious. However, he tirelessly continued his research…

Eventually, we found a dealer who sold "kits" a colossal DIY job to say the least. Where we live - it snows in winter. This vendor guaranteed the snow load.

Done and Done. They delivered the kit, trusses (all metal) and sheets and sheets of metal. After helping him measure and "wrangle" the trusses in place - (literally "wrangle" -I had a rope in each hand as these huge metal forms moved around. Not for the faint of heart!

Rob worked so hard to assemble that carport himself. Screwing each piece together in the hot sun. He was beyond exhausted afterward - he possessed so much purpose when he decided to do something -No rest until the project was done (no matter what that project was).

Looking back, I wonder if his body was already starting to betray him and his mind overrode the warning signs.

So now we had a carport - it worked as it should summer to fall. Winter not so much …

One night, after a long, snowy, exhausting drive back from a neurology appointment—two and a half hours each way—we pulled up our driveway to find the carport COLLAPSED. Snow had crushed it. Crushed our second car. Crushed the trailer. Totaled everything.

That carport was gone. I think something in him collapsed with it. It had been such a labor of love.

He was diagnosed with ALS that previous fall—September 5th. Then the carport crushed in on itself in January. He died June 13th - just five days before our 20th Anniversary. That's not a long time to live with his diagnosis on one hand, on the other it was insufferably long.

However, when you are given a terminal diagnosis, you have zero hope, no thread of a chance at recovery and it weighs so heavy - like living on death row. We knew the ending. We just didn't know how many chapters we had left.

After he passed, I had the life insurance money. Not much. But enough to be dangerous. Did I pay off the house? Pay all credit card debt we had accumulated? Perhaps I realized my income was suddenly cut by over half every month- and set some aside for emergencies?

NOPE.

I did the thing you're never supposed to do: I spent almost all of it on a spectacular carport - really Rob's dream come true for that space. I wish I could say it was practical. It wasn't.

It was purely emotional. A massive, beautifully built roof over those same two containers. Constructed by a good friend. Framed in memory. Paid for by grief. I had a sign made.

It says:

The Rob Geddes Memorial Carport Complete With Deer Skull

"The Rob Geddes Memorial Carport."

The black metal sign hangs on the front -a testimony to love and loss. He would've loved it.

Of course, this would be after he reminded me that I wasn't supposed to spend all the insurance money only months after he passed. It was his vision and that makes me smile every time I go outside.

*Helpful Tip - If you're reading this and walking through your own grief—here's my honest advice:

"Don't make major purchases when your heart is shattered. Especially not with the life insurance. Ask a close friend or relative for their thoughts. Pray about it. Sleep on it. And then sleep on it again, and maybe one more time.

Entry 6 - The Bear Part One & The Bear Part Two

I always knew we lived in bear country. There was a rumor that there had been a grizzly sighting on our property the summer before we started building. Of course, that sounded kinda cool to us in a frontier kind of way.

When Rob heard that, he decided we needed to arm ourselves.

Never in my life did I think I would own a gun, much less use one. So, after a trip to the gun store (that is what they are called, right?), we each had a Judge.

We missed the gun safety class - not the best situation. Rob thought that whenever we were outside we should be packing - He was living his Jeremiah Johnson dream. He wanted to see a bear so badly. Me, not so much.

Of course, one may not live in Montana without owning a rifle - so that was next. I never even tried to shoot that one - the recoil was easy to see and not inviting. I don't understand the fact that people shoot for fun. It's not my cup of tea- it hurts my hand, my ears, and bullets are expensive! I shoot only with purpose and would rather make it to my car and drive off than have a confrontation.

I later ended up with a different pistol with a magazine - it fits my hand much better that the judge. My shooting target is a cookie sheet nailed to a tree. Evidence of my shooting prowess and eagle eye accuracy. (Ha!)

No bear came to visit all the while that Rob was alive. Annie would bark at things in the woods, but, I always thought that it was deer.

The awareness that I'm not really alone in the forest takes on a whole new reality when I found myself solo in the cabin. The Fall after Rob passed, it was 1-2 am and Annie started going BEZERK!

I was going to just open the front door and let her out, but, for some reason I turned on the porch light before I opened the door. Our doors are glass, not the smartest door choice but, it's what we picked. There coming up on the porch was a big BEAR.

I was instantly wide awake - I couldn't believe my eyes. My phone was by the door and I just started snapping pictures as proof. The bear came closer and closer until it was nose to nose with Annie. He looked at us - we looked at him. We had a "moment". Thankfully, we were not of interest to him and he turned around and lumbered off. Adrenaline was pumping throughout every cell, my hands shaking, and yet totally incredulous about what had just happened… My only thought which kept repeating on a loop was "Rob would have loved seeing this bear!"

"The Bear"

THE BEAR (6 Part 2)…

After that first instance, I put up cameras so I would be able to see any other visitors. Sure enough, one walked up and tried to figure out what the camera was up close and personal. Another bear showed up on camera just strolling past my flowers. Typically, I would have been outside watering at the time of that sighting. Thankfully, I only saw those guys on candid camera.

When you find yourself alone in a cabin, outside noises seem that much louder in the dark of night. There was one such night - All of the sudden something was slamming against the side of the cabin. Annie, of course, goes nuts. In a fuzzy sleep state trying to put things together, it didn't register right away what was making all of the ruckus.

I look out of the bedroom window and see my "bear proof garbage can" being dragged off into the woods. The only pause he took was to slam it against the random tree hoping to crack it open and get to the yummy trash inside.

I went back to bed, the garbage can was on it's own. Annie and I stayed safe and sound inside.

The next morning arrived very soon… There were drag marks in the gravel where the bear and can disappeared into the woods. Those were the only indicators that there had been nefarious activity in the night.

Then it hit me, Rob wasn't here to go find the can and potentially find the bear as well.

I had to commence the recovery mission on my own with Annie, and actually take my gun with me. Taking a deep breath, I got out the bullets and loaded the magazine. There was some slight resistance, but, all seemed to go together fine.

Taking a deep breath and saying a quick prayer – I exited through the back door and started making noise as I "tracked" the can. A surprised bear is not a bear I want to find.

Truth be told, I didn't want to find any bear, just my expensive investment of the "bear proof" can.

Annie and I trekked down toward a creek that runs on the property- looking into the woods on either side. My head was "on a swivel". Then, there deep in the trees was the can. That would be the CLOSED, UNBROKEN into can!

The Infamous Certified Bear Proof Garbage Can

I highly, HIGHLY, recommend investing in a certified bear proof garbage can. Not cheap but, worth every nickel.

The bear, however, was nowhere to be seen. Just to be safe, I thought the I would shoot a couple bullets- just to make a noise distraction. and then reclaim the can for my own.

I pulled out my gun, "Click", "Click", no shots fired. There was some resistance when I tried to shoot. "Great," I thought, "Now I need to deal with gun issues." I hiked through the trees, through pretty dense brush, toward my "trophy".

Seeming to have forgotten that this was a FULL garbage can - I try to wrestle it around so I can drag it back up the hill toward where it belonged.

"Wrestle" is the certainly the appropriate word to use here. That thing was heavy, plus the trees were grabbing at me, hiking up uneven ground, up hill was not a fun trip - but, I did it.

Once the can was back in it's place - I had to figure out this gun thing- I pulled the trigger again- nothing. So, it was time to take it apart - I pulled the magazine out, and noticed the bullets looked wrong. They were.

I googled the gun and how to load it. A fully loaded gun with jammed bullets that I repeatedly tried to fire. I LOADED THEM BACKWARDS. Fortunately, the thing didn't explode in my face, or shoot backwards towards me leaving me bleeding or dead.

At that point, I laughed—actually laughed, out loud, alone. The bear was still outside, somewhere. Thinking about that would have to wait for another day.

It hit me then: I wasn't scared of the bear. I was scared of not being enough. Not being strong enough, or Brave enough, or Prepared enough, or Ready enough.

Those experiences also taught me something else-

I might not always be enough. But I am still here and alone a lot of the time-

However, I have a solid community of good friends, true friends that are there for me and just a text or phone call away.

I'm continuing to learn, every day has it's own life lessons.

Rob would be proud of me. I know that truth with every fiber of my being.

Of course, he would shake his head and strongly recommend that I read the gun manual again.

Point Taken…

Entry 7 - You Can Take the Girl Out of Seattle, But You Can't Take Seattle Out of the Girl

My interactions with various forms of wildlife continuously amaze me. Not only that I see them, but, am forced to deal with them on their turf. Gardening (IE planting flowers, and more flowers…and some more, you guessed it flowers), seeing the tiniest green buds growing, the first glimpses of color that herald the coming season of Spring always help my mood. One morning I happened to be cleaning out a garden bed and something made me look up.

The biggest furriest cat I have ever seen was walking nonchalantly across the driveway gravel. I just watched it - then it turned to make eye contact. Very distinct, pointy, furry ears on this big cat's head - screamed "I'm not a cat….I'm a Bobcat!"

I froze but, kept eye contact. Obviously, I was not as interesting to him as he was to me. He continued his sauntering across the gravel and into the woods.

That was a new one.

Rob would've been thrilled at this new native species.

"Bobcat"

Entry 8 - Weird Things I Have Found On My Porch

I woke up one morning, was getting breakfast, and some very strong black tea when I looked out the front door and had to blink hard.

There, right outside the front door, was a perfectly severed deer leg. Just one. Frozen solid. Hoof and all. I'm sure at some point this scene was in a B listed horror movie.

Annie had apparently dragged it back as a gift, or a snack for later - she looked at me like " Impressive, huh?".

I was pretty taken aback - I never had a full deer part to deal with before. I just turned around and proceeded to put it out of my mind - it was breakfast time after all (also in the back of my mind I strongly hoped it would vanish).

It didn't. I didn't scream. I didn't cry. I didn't even really flinch. I just stared at it —this grotesque, bizarre token of wildness—and thought:

"Really Rob? This is your job- your dog, your problem"…

Frustrated and disgusted - I knew it was now - "My dog, my problem".

the mystery surrounding where the rest of the deer was, came the following Spring. My friend was over helping me with some things and he walked over to me and said

"Do you know there is a full deer carcass behind your propane tank. (Sans leg)?"

"Uh nope".

He told me that the head with antlers was still there - Now, I'm not a hunter - this is the only kind of "trophy" I will most likely ever get. He helped it get to where it is a blanched out and ready for next step.

That bleached out skull with antlers hangs right under the "Rob Geddes Memorial Carport" sign. It's not a skull most would put up, but, for me it works.

The current future I am living is not the future I imagined with Rob in Montana. I was cheated out of that. This is not a situation I asked for, never planned for, and certainly was not the way our lives were supposed to go.

But, it is the way life DID go. More adjusting….

Living alone in the woods teaches you a few things.

One: Wildlife does not care about your comfort.

Two: You can, in fact, handle more than you think.

Three: Sometimes, the only thing to do is follow

Elizabeth Taylor's advice:

"Pour yourself a drink, put on some lipstick, and pull yourself together."

Along with the aforementioned Bobcat and Deer leg, there was another front porch surprise.

To fully appreciate the significance of that other discovery, I need to give you some back story.

Entry 9 - Fear of Birds… Aviary PTSD is REAL

It started with a rooster.

I was five. Maybe six. My Grandma and Grandpa lived on a piece of land with a few chickens—just enough to feel like you were in the country, not enough to justify the trauma.

This rooster was not your friendly cartoon chicken. He was a beady-eyed, flapping, spur-wielding demon. His domain was a non issue for me until…

One morning, I went outside to get something, like I'd been told. Upon my stepping onto the porch, that rooster launched himself at me like a feathered missile. Wings out, claws forward, screaming whatever foul profanity roosters scream when they attack.

I was trapped between the screen door and the house. My Grandpa heard the commotion, stepped on the porch and drop kicked that rooster across the yard.

After concluding that I was not fatally injured, my Grandma tried to figure out what caused the attack. Come to find out a dish of dry cat food on the porch - the rooster probably thought I had come outside to take his food -hence, the violence that has affected me throughout my entire life. Bird PTSD. It's a thing.

My bird fear does not end with roosters - it is any feathered beaked being.

There are wild turkeys everywhere around where I live. Huge birds - I have even had "turkey vultures" spend the night in front of my kitchen window. Like regular turkeys, only bigger and uglier. It was winter, I have no idea what made them decide to camp there. There was 8 or 9 of them - all sleeping on one leg with their heads tucked under their wing. Terrifying - I yelled to get them to move on, nothing. Then I called out the big guns, Annie. She went out and was barking up a storm. I watched from the window, expecting a flurry while they tried to get away - nope. They slowly untucked their heads, put their other foot down, and then went slowly down my driveway. Freaky.

Turkey Vultures Outside My Kitchen Window - "Sleeping"

Here in Heron, Montana, I live literally surrounded by birds. Hummingbirds swarm my feeders. Finches gossip in the trees. Woodpeckers hammer out Morse code on the side of my house.

My first woodpecker experience was interesting. I was inside doing something creative or whatever. "Knock Knock Knock". Annie lifted her head - obviously I had company. I look on the porch, around the driveway - nothing. So, I sat down again

The Only Time I'm Not Terrified

"Knock Knock Knock". This was getting weird. Thinking that the answer might be outside, I stepped out and looked at the cabin. There was a woodpecker - about 12 inches high, going crazy on the cedar siding. One plus one typically equals two - Woodpecker - makes holes in wood. Cabin - all . There's wood siding. Equals - holes in my house.

It was obviously a 911 cabin emergency. I went inside and, you guessed it, grabbed my gun, and

went outside. (Bullets correctly loaded). Of course, I had.

"This is when the beady eyes and pointy beaks start to terrify me" -

No more climbing the ladder for me!"

My closest neighbor I knew had her chickens gated, but, on the off chance Annie got one - I called her after I saw it there.

I told her about the disappearing chicken - she didn't think it was one of hers and I didn't give that much thought.

Then when it disappeared, I called back to let her know -

She said, "Oh, my son came up and got it."

Well, alright then - another one for the books.

Side Note...

When we bought the property the paperwork noted: "No birds. No fowl. No exceptions." Obviously, that chicken was trespassing and paid a hefty price. Hopefully, the word is out and there will be no further instances.

I'm not going to hold my breath - I have learned to expect the unexpected.

Plus - Regarding the original rooster incident—I'm still not over it.

Entry 10 - There Is a Mouse In My House

Another foreign invader from the forest is that of field mice. I had never had the "pleasure" of having a mouse in my house growing up. I had never had the joy of waking up in the middle of the night to a "scratching like they were digging their way to China" sound. Or, the distinctive squeal of a little furry visitor that was being chased by cats, and finding "evidence" of their visit (FYI those are NOT sesame seeds") until Cabin Life. The battle for a mouse free existence commenced - and, yet still continues. I feel like they were trying to retain, or reclaim, their territory. As I have mentioned, Phrank was the Master Mouser. Phloyd could care less - he was a lover, not a fighter.

The fall after Rob passed - after Phloyd and Phrank had passed as well, I adopted an orange cat - Phred. The following Spring I rescued Phrieda, a long hair tabby. Then the following winter, a Siamese, Phoebe joined the ranks. I am saddened to report there is not a mouser among them.

(By now you may have recognized a pattern in cat names - nope, not a typo - they all start with "PH" instead of the traditional "F". We started with Phloyd, and the tradition continues…)

One morning I woke up and all of my coffee table books were a mess on the floor. All three cats were sitting among the books and just looked at me. So I shrugged, put the books back, and didn't think a lot about it. That evening sitting on the couch all three cats were together doing "something". I got up to see what the fuss was about…

The cats were PLAYING with a mouse. By "playing", I mean grabbing the live mouse, then letting it go, flipping it around, in an extended game of cat and mouse. Yikes!

The mouse ran under the kitchen island and was inaccessible. The cats just sort of walked around the island once and lost interest. I missed my expert mouser, Phrank. He was no player. Results were what I wanted - not games.

They caught and lost, caught and lost the crazy mouse. What a sick game of catch and release! I had a fear that they were going to bring their new toy up on the bed when I was sleeping. Some days went by with me seeing the mouse dart from under a table, up a curtain, and be MIA after that. "On edge" are the words I would use to describe the mood in the cabin.

About a week later, I had an appointment in town. But, before I left I told those cats, *all three of them", that I better come home to a dead mouse or, there would be no dinner for any of them.

They actually listened. FINALLY! They did their job and I filled my end of the bargain, I fed them.

Needless to say they perhaps are not the smartest felines I have had the pleasure of knowing. My "PHun" cats have since gone back to thinking mice are playthings.

Trying to train them to hunt is absolutely still a work in progress, like everything else in my life.

Entry 11 - The Invasion

My last entry under this topic of wayward wildlife - is: Invasion.

Spring was just about to really get underway. I was standing at the bathroom sink , washing my face, and all at once black ants started pouring, I MEAN POURING, through EVERY door sill, knot hole, and crevice you can imagine.

I had NO bug spray on hand. I rapidly googled what will kill ants - white vinegar and baking soda. Great! So I run around and collect every box of baking soda from the refrigerator, freezer, cabinet and then located a bottle and a half of white vinegar. I was in business!

I threw down the baking soda over the ants, followed by a thorough dousing of white vinegar. I was not stingy with either. The concoction slowed them down but, this was right out of a horror movie. Hitchcock could not have written a more scary scene.

When I had coated about every surface I could find, I thought I had at least won "a" battle - maybe. Then thinking that I was, if not totally, the victor, at least a winning soldier, I went to bed. After I dozed off, I woke up suddenly to a very foreign feeling -it was revenge of the black ants. They were crawling ON MY FACE!

I don't recommend waking up that way.

Terrified and repulsed. I placed an early morning "exterminator rescue 911" call. He could come out in a day - I hoped that I could keep them at bay that long.

There was only one more box of baking soda left. Research yielded some natural methods of anti-anting - including "Cinnamon" and "Pepper". I added whole bottles of those things to the vinegar and baking soda concoction. It's white pasty cemented substance was complete with a myriad of ants encased like Han Solo in Carbonate.

Trying to eradicate the dead ants, hardened baking soda and vinegar, with a cinnamon/pepper twist was NOT easy AT ALL. Google never said anything about that difficulty. To this day I still see traces of that baking soda paste in corners.

I absolutely do NOT recommend this solution.

I find it worth every penny to have the exterminator visit in the Spring and Fall religiously.

Entry 12 - The Ark

You know how a great survival experience includes a figurative "Ark"?

I ask you to think back a few entries to what the "carport" needed to cover- a 40' x 40' x 40' x 40' space (two containers spaced 40' across).

We moved here with those two 40 foot containers and also two 20 foot containers. They were referred to collectively as "The Ark".

We were moving from an over 3,000 square foot house, and also close to that size "barn". No animals for the barn -just classic cars, assorted storage, and heavy equipment in there.

The Cabin is about 1,100 square feet. You can do the math. So, we had to decide what would come with us to our next chapter in Montana. Hence began the sorting and figuring out what was going to go on the "ark" to Montana.

Not an easy task. Especially for two sentimental pack rats like Rob and I.

It was brutal. I had to leave some of my favorite antique pieces of furniture behind. Antiquing was a huge hobby of ours over the years and we had the collections that backed that statement up.

The moving sale we had prior to moving was huge. Our leather couches and chairs, my antique French hunting cabinet, a dresser, office roll top desk, and everything else that goes with that were up for discussion.

Before we moved, I had an extremely large, user friendly kitchen that was actually fun to cook in, and the cabinets… oh, those cabinets…(I miss them and I miss my dishwasher). That might sound superficial - but, it's honest.

So we packed our stuff into the containers and moved on over to Montana. Kinda like the Beverly Hillbillies.

We were strangers to the many changes, or, fully comprehend the differences between life in western Washington and Montana. We definitely were not prepared for the magnitude of difference and nuanced experiences that we would encounter.

When I do something now that doesn't make sense, or mess up on something native Montanans know from birth - I shrug and say "my Washington roots are showing".

These containers were always something we knew we needed to go through and sort the contents. However, something always came up - family, finances, etc… and proved to be a distraction away from things that we had planned to accomplish in our new chapter. Regardless, things rapidly filled up our lives and the containers sat. The covering of the containers took precedence over sorting the contents. Then when Rob got sick they continued to sit, like sealed time capsules -and the containers sat, and they sat…

They were time capsules from our past life, a testimony to great trips, memories, laughter, and tears. I was afraid of them actually. Afraid at all "the feels" that would go with opening them and knowing would need to be processed emotionally. Knowing full well the physical toll that this project would take was daunting to say the least. Packing them in the first place was tough enough and we were doing it together. The knowledge that I was going to be tackling them alone was paralyzing. I needed a catalyst.

One day I noticed a Facebook post that there would be a community yard sale in downtown Heron. Downtown consists of a small store, post office, and marijuana dispensary - (don't try and say that we out here in the country aren't progressive).

This seemed like an awesome opportunity to sell some of the excess, and make some extra funds that always seem to be needed.

So, in order to access things to sell, I had to vanquish the "Container".

I opened the side door…Have you ever seen an episode of Hoarders? Well, I found a container that belonged on the show. It was packed tight with books, papers, tools, toys, a 1971 dirt bike, some furniture, a couple saddles, camping stuff… just soooo much!

The smell hit me first - the mouse pee, mold, decomposing rodents, and general smell of rot. Wow, just Wow. How was I ever going to clear any of it out, and was it even worth tackling?

A friend of mine had loaned me their covered trailer to put stuff for the sale in - However, in order for me to put anything in there is needed to be cleaned, repaired if possible, and in sell-able condition.

So I took a breath (before I went near the container), said a prayer, and started eating that elephant one bite at a time. Shortly after taking a few bags out, I began a running conversation with Rob. We were supposed to go through this mess together. Well, there was only me left so- BINGO.

Seeing things that we thought were packed away, protected and safe, - crushed and ruined. Opening a tub and finding that a creature had made a home - not only for themselves, but for a few subsequent generations as well. I was somewhere between grief, anger, sadness, frustration, and a riot of other emotions.

Side note- I had always thought a pack rat was just someone who didn't want to throw things away, silly me. They are real and their nests are INSANE. They start at one spot and just keep building and stashing and building and stashing all kinds of nastiness. That was freaky to come across.

Nothing was sacred, or safe. Let's just say I was not about to reach into ANY area without gloves and clear field of vision.

I started laughing - not a ha ha laugh, more of a lunatic fringe/losing it laugh. It soon turned to tears and yelling at Rob for leaving me with this colossal mess, leaving me alone, forcing me to do things that I never imagined I would deal with in a million years.

I spent hours that initial day going down a memory lane rabbit hole. If things couldn't be saved with a Clorox wipe - I had to say goodbye. Not my strong suit. Photos that had not made it into albums were stashed in boxes in no particular order - from old company dinner photos, all the things from Rob's office, to my books. I mean lots of BOOKS ruined or damaged in some way.

When my stepson helped me move into Rob's house the week before we got married, he hauled the many boxes of my books - heavy boxes up a small ladder into the attic in our first house. He periodically brought it up - as in - "Do you really need all of these?"

Let's just say I have always been a reader- for example, I read Gone With the Wind in 2nd grade. I am not a fan of checking books out of a library because they have to be returned. I like the option being available to me to read my favorites over and over So the short answer was "Yes, I really needed all of them".

Well, those boxes of: expensive hardback editions, cookbooks, crafting books, gardening books, romance novels, mental health books, religious books, and more -were really hard for me to sort through and find them damaged. What was even worse was finding cards and letters from people long gone, destroyed/unreadable. It was like losing loved ones all over again. Every time I couldn't clean something, or had to throw a memory away it hurt more than I expected - But, I had to remember that there is an unmarred memory locked away in my heart where no damage can reach it.

Not only had I saved every note Rob had ever written me - from paper towels to post it notes- he had saved the ones from me. They had all been carefully put in boxes and sent over to Montana on the "ark". These were not exempt from the carnage, no matter how much I wished differently, it was what it was.

When I tell you Rob was sentimental, I mean it. For example, I had to leave a few favorite (but large) pieces of furniture behind - "there was no room on the ark".

Then lo and behold, what did I find? BOXES upon boxes of schoolwork - for each of his kids - a box for each grade with their name on it. They were all ruined - feeding a fire is about the only thing they could be good for at this point. Sad - but, reality.

There were items I came across that were too large or heavy for me to solo handle. A helping hand was needed and appreciated.

There is a couple that lives in town, and are part of my local congregation - they have been priceless and unflinching in helping me with a variety of things that have happened and continue to crop up. Gary, who built the carport, has been vital in helping me with the big stuff. My dear friend, his wife - Sharon, has been emotionally there and physically - going to town appointments with me when they are far away, and just being there. Knowing those two are in my corner has really helped me in so many ways. I cannot imagine going through losing Rob without them and the rest of my local community/congregation.

When Rob and I discovered Heron, we were on a 3 week, multiple states, into the Canadian Rockies, and more bike ride. (Motorcycle of Course…)

Two Up - One of our favorite hobbies…

We were riding on a sunny day on Highway 200 - past Lake Ponderay, beautiful forests and clean air - I was even using my phone to film a video for a bit. Rob had turned sideways and said "We've got to move here." This was the first time he had EVER said anything like that. My response surprised both of us. I said, "Yes we do".

Since our faith is a huge part of who we are - we were wondering about the location of the closest Kingdom Hall in relation to this paradisaical area we had discovered. We asked that question out loud, then we looked to our right -

BOOM! There it was- about 10 minutes from the town that we had just declared was to be our next chapter. Throughout the rest of our trip we excitedly discussed the idea and execution of this new and exciting plan that was quickly taking place.

Follow through is one of the things that I loved about Rob. I'm certain we all know people who have great ideas but, that is where they stay, "idea land". When Rob had a plan or an idea, it was as good as done. He would do all the research and figure out how to make it work. That was where the "idea" for our move was currently at - "research", soon it would graduate to "plan", then "execution".

I continued to plow through the containers one item at a time. Soon, one was half empty, three quarters empty - one finally was sorted… three to go….

The stench in the containers was so invasive it seemed burned into every fiber of my being -

Three showers later, and with a load of heavy duty laundry transferred to the dryer… I was ready to call it a day.

The yard sale trailer was full and ready to go.

Progress…deep breath (outside air) … Yes, Progress.

Grief is a fluid thing. One minute you are yelling because you are alone, next you are reading a legal pad with his handwriting, and can hear him talking to you in a voice that has ceased to be heard, but that is familiar and dear as if you had just hung up the phone after hearing the person you love most -tell you how much he loves you back.

I love you
Brandi's Geddes
Forever-
You & Me
The Truest of
love-
Reece A. Geddes

Needs no Caption - This note says it all…

Entry 13 - The Weight On One Set of Hands

There's a kind of tired that seeps into your bones when you realize—it's all on you now.

It's not just the grief. It's not just the silence. It's the fact that if something breaks, you fix it. If something leaks, you figure it out. If something needs lifting, moving, shoveling, sorting, re-routing, re-wiring, or re-imagining—well, guess who?

I was not raised to fix plumbing. Or reset fuses. Or troubleshoot the terrifying mystery of septic tanks.

Winter is a historically stressful season. Little did I know that I was going to need to do something with septic.

One early evening, I heard some horrific gurgling in the pipes. Not exactly what you want to hear as your day is wrapping up. Gurgling is never good. Especially in the pipes. ESPECIALLY when no one else is around to go, "Huh - that's weird, Can you google what to do, or what is the top cause of that sound?" Then it gets worse…way worse. After the last deep pipe noise- water/sewage started backing up through the bathtub drain, the shower drain, spare bathroom drain, sinks everywhere backed up with what they should never ever back up with.

I took a deep breath, counted to 5 (no time to make it all the way to 10), and called Gary- I had no idea if something had burst, or what disaster was brewing in unseen spaces.

A bad side effect of downsizing is that you use any and all space you can find for storage- I mean ANY space. For example, a bathtub, an unused shower stall - all are great storage places until those places that were back up storage spaces- Back Up!.

Definitely not an ideal situation. (Understatement!)

A rapid-rescue mission of the stored treasures commenced - Where do you move all the things that have been put in safe storage spaces? When those things are no longer safe, a riot of emotions again came knocking, and I had no choice but to go through everything - again. "Sort, Wash, and Toss"- a new Mantra.

One step forward, three steps back.

Gary opened the septic lid, cleared the clog, and things started going toward the drain field again. Here's the practical, but embarrassing reason for the catastrophe that I needed to clean up. He asked me a pretty personal question - "Do you use the extra double/triple layer toilet paper?" Odd, but OK.

It was towards the end of COVID - Maybe he needed to borrow some?!

"Sure…why?" I replied.

Well, here's the learning moment…

When living with a septic system - there are certain products that can perhaps clog the pipe - especially in winter.

I.E. Do not flush thick toilet paper EVERY time you go to the bathroom. "Number one" should be deposited into a small covered garbage can beside the toilet, while "Number two" can be flushed. This dramatically reduces the amount of paper the pipes have to process, thereby reducing the chances of things backing up. Plus, do not run laundry (Back to Back to Back) and take a shower. Makes the quantity of water the pipes have to deal with an overload. Again - smart advice. I immediately instituted these new "house rules". There has not been a gurgling pipe since. Whew!

Being here by myself has given me an education -parts of it I could have done without (similar to how I felt about P.E class in school). I now "try" to view things that come up, things that I need to do, or need to learn, as continuing education. Sometimes it works - sometimes not.

When power to the front room lights goes out, but, lights on everywhere else? Check the fuse panel. I have become very familiar with the fuse panel - they go out, I flip the switch, power comes back on.

You are your own I.T. person. WiFi out? - Plug and Unplug the modem (they always tell you to do that first). Now you can tell the cell phone or WiFi people that you already did the first thing they always tell you to do. This might save you a few extra minutes of phone time with your new friend that speaks English as a second language in Customer Service. Even if English is a first language for the customer service rep on the help line, it can still take hours of your life to clear up any tech issues.

As one of your animals gets older and older, they just aren't themselves. Perhaps they are doing something they have never done before… It's on you, as the last "responsible pet owner" in the house, to make the tough, heartbreaking call to end their suffering.

There is no back up opinion, no one to come home to, and no one to share memories and tears with you.

Taking Phloyd for that final ride was one of the hardest things I have ever done. He was the closet thing to a child that Rob and I had. That was not a call that I wanted to make alone- but, I did.

When Annie's health goes, that will also be especially hard. She is the last surviving animal that I have now that "knew" Rob. But, that day is not today. I will cross that bridge when I absolutely have to.

All different kinds and degrees of emotional and physical weight - they both are now in your set of hands, one set of hands.

I have had moments of crisis, moments of joy, moments of melancholy, moments where the loss feels like a tsunami wave engulfing me, and moments of quiet. All of those moments I own - they are woven into the fabric that is me.

I do have animated conversations, sometimes in my thoughts and sometimes aloud, with Rob about all those things - swearing, sweating, and dealing with the random wildlife (inside and out). I think on the things he has not been present for. I do wonder what he would have thought of COVID along with a score of other events that have happened in the world, with family, loss of friends, getting to know new ones…

Yet, in the midst of all of that - there are moments of pride, of grit and determination, I feel in those moments like I have earned the right to declare myself a true Montanan.

Elizabeth Bennett from Pride and Prejudice when she said -

"My courage always rises with every attempt to intimidate me."

Sure, I get that the character Jane Austin created was set in historical England but, the principle still bears itself out here in my cabin, on my mountain in Montana.

I also think of my favorite Bible verse - 1 Corinthians 10:13

"No temptation has come upon you except what is common to men. But God is faithful, and he will not let you be tempted beyond what you can bear, but along with the temptation he will also make the way out so that you may endure it."

Mother Teresa paraphrased the above verse by saying…

"I know God won't give me anything I can't handle. I just wish he didn't trust me so much."

In hindsight, I probably should have started a notebook citing each challenge at the time I went through it - What it was and how I survived it. Of course, I have the accounts recorded in this book which are all accurate. (Which I can assure you are by no means complete- A sequel in the works? Who knows…)

After I am gone, I can only hope that my Grandson finds this book, is proud of me for being who I am, for facing each and every challenge and for never giving up on our dream. He will be the one, the only one, who will inherit his Grandpa Rob and Grandma Brandi's legacy and that makes me happy. Rob loved him very VERY much. I likewise love our Grandson, have always loved him, and will continue to very much until my last breath. Knowing he will have access to our story, (and subsequently my solo story, & struggles) holds a very special place in my heart. I pray he is able to appreciate this Montana treasure, and will build his own story of grit, determination, and love on top of ours.

The Cabin

There is a strange satisfaction in knowing that at 8:00pm when I turn the lights out it will have been a day lived to the very best of my ability. I can sleep with the knowledge that I have survived and thrived another day. Then, the next day's unforeseen challenges come, and I confidently, or maybe not so confidently, still get up, face them, and learn new lessons and ways of doing things that I didn't even know that I didn't know.

The Sun Sets at Day's End

Entry 14 - Grief Is Not a Straight Line

I wish grief came with a set of instructions, a road map, spread sheet, or, better yet- a calendar.

The calendar would have an alert that said,

"Here, this week here - you'll be OK," and

"Next Tuesday at 11:18am you will fall apart - plan accordingly."

But no. Grief doesn't call ahead, or RSVP. Grief shows up unannounced and in hiking boots tracking hunks of mud all over your carefully cleaned heart.

One day you are doing fine, smiling and maybe even laughing. Then the next day you are crying in the grocery store because your wedding song just came across the music system.

Grief is not a straight line. Grief is a drunken loop. Grief is a roller coaster, the kind that slams you back in your seat when it takes off and then leaves you stuck hanging upside down. Grief is like a squirrel hopped up on coffee beans. Grief is different for every person.

Sometimes I miss Rob with a dull ache in my heart. Sometimes it's like a fire poker to the chest. And then sometimes, it's just the quiet missing of something I cannot put to words. Like I've lost the missing word of a well know quote, spent hours trying to find a familiar place, finally stop and ask directions then even with that assistance, can no longer find that special place.

There is no explaining the grief journey to people. Most don't even really want to hear you try. Not because they don't care- but, because they are uncomfortable, and not sure how to act or what to say. They would prefer a cleaned up version of loss- like a closed box tied with string. The whole "look how strong you are" version of loss. The movie montage with soft piano music and a perfectly timed sunrise.

A brave woman I know has been navigating her new situation, after losing her beloved husband. She made a Facebook post which really resonated with me. It showed a campfire, nice, burning really well with two chairs by it. She posted "my husband and I always enjoyed sitting out here by the fire" so, he's here.

I thought that was so sweet because it is important to do things that make you remember and give you happy memories. Those memories are vital - that is just how we as human beings cope.

The more we love the deeper we grieve. It's been six years since I have lost Rob - in those six years there is not a not a day that he is out of my mind and heart. Sometimes I see something that he would find funny - I smile. Just having him to talk to, or joke with, is one of the biggest things I miss. Some days I am laughing. Some days I'll pull out a photo album, and it's ok. I miss him every day in so many different ways. For myself it has been vitally important to remember things we used to do together and enjoy - now I am doing them alone, with the memory of him ever present.

Memories surround me - and when reminiscing on those special things and events, they keep Rob, in a sense, here. Of course, I have photos of us all over the cabin - it makes him here. I have a sign that he bought me that says "I made a wish and you came true." That sign hangs on my wall - I'll never take it down.

Grief is not cinematic. It is messy. It's ugly crying into a pillow at 3:00 am. It's manic cleaning the kitchen. It's laughing at a Netflix series he would have hated - then feeling guilty about it.

It's finding a t-shirt in the back of the closet you can't toss. Grief is listening on repeat a voicemail that will never be deleted. Perhaps a song you can't bring yourself to listen to, but, that you absolutely must listen to.

Grief could be described as the never ending battle to make peace with the fact that you will never make peace with the loss of your best friend, your person.

That is okay.

There are days I feel strong. Capable. Even joyful.

There are days I am a shadow on a cloudy day -Desperately needing the sun to come out to make me visible.

Time has passed -sometimes it seems like yesterday, sometimes it seems like I have been without my light, my Sunshine, forever.

I have learned to stop "judging" my days, or force these unique days of life into someone else's mold…Instead, I let them be what the days be what they are.

Grief is not a straight line. However, it is mine.

I am traveling this loopy line the very best I can… Just as I know, beyond a doubt, that every single person who has faced horrible loss, is grieving- traveling on their own individual grief line.

The very best way I can describe what this kind of loss is this illustration.

Have you ever seen two trees that wind around and around each other until it is hard to see where one ends and the other begins? Now imagine one of those trees being forcefully ripped away - the remaining tree is still there - scarred permanently and not as strong as when the two trees were together.

I often feel like the remaining tree - I might bloom in the Spring, but, I will never flourish in the same strong way as we did when we were "two trees" together.

I will get stronger bit by bit and learn to bloom in different ways - although always knowing that half of me is missing, and will never grow back.

So much stronger together ... but, still standing as one.

I certainly do not fault people who decide to move on to another relationship or marriage with someone else after losing their spouse. There are some who go on to marry multiple people. (Consecutively, of course) I've seen some very happy couples that have made that decision. However, That is not me. There will not be anyone new in my life - there is no room in that special place in my heart - Rob still owns it and always will.

Entry 15 - Summary, Notes on Survival With a Soapbox Closer…

Love hard. Give 150% - you will never regret it.

However, You will regret it, if you are not loving like that .

Grieve in your own way. Smile when you can. Cry when you need to. Let the memories be treasures, not burdens.

Be kind -Everyone is going through something.

Don't hoard something because it's on sale - Grief is ALWAYS on sale, don't hoard that either.

Let go of expectations people have for what they think your life should look like now.

Let go of timelines and tidy endings. Grief has neither. There is no calendar event you can draw a line through, or a milestone you can reach. It is a thread woven into and through your life now - sometimes loose and fluttering, sometimes pulled so tight you cannot breathe.

Out of the clutter find simplicity.

There is beauty in the mess and strength in the quiet.

There is comfort in the smallest moments - a cat curled up on your chest, the way snow sparkles when the sun shines on it, a memory that makes you laugh out loud while washing dishes.

Lean on your faith, your Creator, true friends, and your own quiet strength.

Some practical things I have learned is - you do not have to panic over a medical, or any other kind, of bill. Call, ask, negotiate. You'd be surprised at how often the answer is yes. Check if your new income (or lack thereof) makes you eligible for property tax reduction, or different county, federal, or state benefits. That is what they are there for.

Buy what you need and use what you have.

Go outside. Every season has a gift for us. Fall's warm tones, Spring's tender promise. Summer's full bloom of reward. The quiet hush that prevails after Winter's first (and subsequent) snow.

"Soapbox Alert"…

There is a word, title that is found in the English language. I loathe it. I ask you to make for yourself a mental image, one that you get in your mind when you hear the word "widow".

Do you envision an old lady, unable to walk upright, hard of hearing, poor, who relies on everyone for everything as if it was a right that she inherited at the loss of her spouse? I have always not liked that word, I will tell you why.

Throughout my life I have known many women who have found themselves without their spouse. They have been the strongest most interesting women I have ever met. Never bowing to the stereotypes that their situation conjures up.

As a whole, they have the most interesting stories, exciting experiences, and such intelligent and wry senses of humor. Those are who I hold as examples of survival in the face of great loss. I want people who I know - younger or older, to think of me that way as well. I want to be seen as a Survivor.

With the loss of my Husband, I have a renewed sense of appreciation for how strong these women were. I can understand the aloneness they must have felt at different times. If it is a circumstance you have not personally experienced, trust me you do not understand. Don't say that you do. Please be kind - everyone grieves differently.

I would like to propose we eradicate from our language the term "widow".

Instead, let's call ourselves "Survivors".

Because, that is what, and who we are.

My parting thought is "Focus on the step in front, not the whole staircase."

Entry 16 - About the Author

Brandis Geddes - "Survivor"

Brandis Geddes is a Montana-based photographer, writer, and artist who lives in a cabin nestled on twenty acres of forest in Heron, Montana. She specializes in nature photography—sunrises, scenic views, brilliant floral macros, and quiet animal moments—often capturing beauty from unexpected angles. After the loss of her husband Rob to Bulbar ALS, she turned her grief into art, building a creative life surrounded by color, memory, and meaning.

She shares her cabin with Annie the dog and three beloved cats: Phred, Phrieda, and Phoebe—her daily sources of chaos and comfort.

You can view her work online at: www.brandisgart.com

www.ingramcontent.com/pod-product-compliance
Lightning Source LLC
Chambersburg PA
CBHW070101100426
42743CB00012B/2620